Walk 1:- Lower Falls Riverside W~~~~ ~ ~

Start - Stile at side of bridge G.R.145684
Distance - 2.4km (1.5miles)   **Time to allo**
Parking - In parking area near Bridge. (Low
Terrain - Grass, stony path
Comment - A good introduction to Glen Nevi
of the area.

GW00738697

1. After parking your car, walk to the bridge nearby. At the side there is a stile, cross and continue walking upstream along the riverbank.
2. You start to ascend slightly through woodland nearby the river.
3. Look to your left by the river, when you are on higher ground, for a small bridge which takes you back across the river to the road at G.R.159684.
4. At the road turn left walking for 1.4km back to the car park.

Walk 2:- The Wishing Stone/Forest Walk (circular)

Start/Parking - Last car park on the left before leaving the Glen G.R.122737
Distance - 2.5km (1.55miles)   **Time to allow** - 45 minutes
Terrain - Easy walk on a track and path with only a short ascent.
Comment - This walk can incorporate a visit to Glen Nevis Visitor Centre. There are good views of the Ben path leading up from the Visitor Centre and of the Glen itself.

1. From the car park, descend the short distance to the main road then turn right walking for 1km on the footpath to a sign on your right pointing to The West Highland Way along a short path between fields. Before you arrive there you pass a large wishing stone at the side of the footpath, which has a plaque near it. You then pass the entrance to Glen Nevis Visitor Centre on your left before you reach The West Highland Way sign on your right.
2. Turn onto this path walking for 120m to a kissing gate which you go through then ascend a short distance to a wide forest track running left to right.
3. Turn right at this point. A sign points left to The West Highland Way but you should turn right.
4. Keep on the wide track through the forest on a general bearing of 18°M for 1.1km, which leads back to the car park where you originally started from.

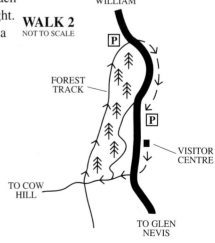

Walk 3:- Glen Nevis Short Riverside Walk (circular)

Start/Parking - Glen Nevis Visitor Centre G.R. 123730

Distance - 3.2km (2miles)   Time to Allow - 50minutes

Terrain - Flat path, easy to follow.

Comment - A nice relaxing walk along the riverbank with clear water in the River Nevis flowing swiftly to the sea. The kids will enjoy this walk.

1. After parking at the Visitor Centre car park, pick up the path along by the river near the entrance. Walk on this path away from the Visitor Centre towards Fort William in a northerly direction to the suspension bridge.

2. Cross the bridge following the sign to 'Ben path'. Continue on this path along the riverbank passing Achintee Farm (B&B) on your left. You can see the Visitor Centre on the opposite side of the river.

3. At a turning left for the Ben path, carry straight on along by the river do not take the path off to the left. You should now see the Glen Nevis camping park on the opposite side of the river as you progress on this flat path.

4. Cross four burns running into the river before coming to a footbridge spanning the River Nevis.

5. Cross this bridge where you should see the Glen Nevis Youth Hostel opposite.

6. Turn right crossing the road onto the footpath and walking for 1.4km, passing a white house (B&B) then an entrance to The West Highland Way on the left before crossing the road and going through an entrance into the Glen Nevis Visitor Centre again.

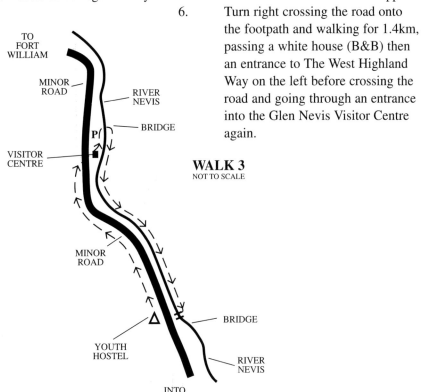

WALK 3
NOT TO SCALE

Walk 4 :- Nevis Forest Walk (circular)

Start/Parking - Glen Nevis Visitor Centre G.R.123730
Distance - 3.3km (2 miles)　　　**Time to allow - 50minutes**
Terrain - Easy walk on a good path with a short ascent.
Comment - A pleasant walk with good views of Glen Nevis

1. Leave the Visitor Centre by turning left along the Glen Nevis road into the Glen then walk for 1.1km to the Glen Nevis Restaurant on the opposite side of the road.
2. Turn right where a small sign for The West Highland Way points along the metalled road.
3. Walk between the houses at the far end of the road, bear left onto a stony path near a small garage.
4. Walk through a kissing gate beside a 5 bar gate leading into the forest, where a sign on the gate states 'walkers welcome here'. Ascend for a short distance to a wider track running left to right.
5. Turn right here then soon after a path joins from the left, but continue straight ahead for 700m to a waymark sign.
6. Turn right, down to a kissing gate then onto the main road 120m further on.
7. Turn left at the road then right soon after, through a narrow opening taking you back into Glen Nevis Visitor Centre.

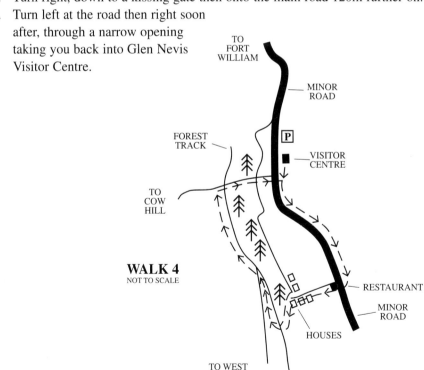

Walk 5:- Ben Path Walk (circular)
Start/Parking - Glen Nevis Visitor Centre G.R. 123730
Distance - 5.8km (3.6miles)   Time to allow - 1½hours
Terrain - Easy walk on a good path with a short ascent.
Comment - A good walk with excellent views along the Glen

1. Leaving the Glen Nevis Visitor Centre entrance, walk on the path along by the river in a northerly direction to the suspension bridge nearby.
2. Cross the bridge following the Ben path sign. Continue on the obvious path for 360m, passing Achintee Farm (B&B) on your left. The Visitor Centre is now on the opposite side of the river.
3. You come to some steps over the fence and another sign pointing to 'Ben path'. Cross here walking up a straight path for 250m to some steps in a stone wall.
4. Climb over the wall steps then cross a farm track ascending on a stony path bearing right towards Ben Nevis. You have good views along the Glen in both directions.
5. You ascend for 900m then join another path rising steeply from the right.
6. Turn right here and descend to the bridge over the river and the youth hostel on the far side. While descending you may see the youth hostel in the Glen below. Take care on the steep path. Just before the river is an information board giving weather conditions on Ben Nevis.
7. Cross the bridge to the youth hostel then turn right, taking care in crossing, then walk for 1.4km back to Glen Nevis Visitor Centre. Pass the entrance to the camping park on your left then a white house (B&B) then an entrance to The West Highland Way on the left.
8. Cross the road here towards the river and go through an opening into the Visitor Centre again.

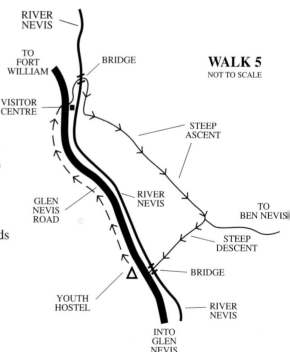

RIVER NEVIS

TO FORT WILLIAM

BRIDGE

WALK 5
NOT TO SCALE

VISITOR CENTRE

STEEP ASCENT

GLEN NEVIS ROAD

RIVER NEVIS

TO BEN NEVIS

STEEP DESCENT

BRIDGE

YOUTH HOSTEL

RIVER NEVIS

INTO GLEN NEVIS

Walk 6:- Cow Hill Mast (height 278m)

Start/Parking - Glen Nevis Visitor Centre G.R.123730

Distance - 5.8km (3.6 miles)   Time to allow - 1¾hours

Terrain - Very steep ascent and descent for 750m on a well-defined path

Comment - This is one of the harder walks but well worth the effort. Ensure you have some extra warm clothing to put on at the summit.

1. Turn left out of the Visitor Centre car park, cross with care, walk for 230m to an entrance leading to The West Highland Way.

2. Turn right here, a small sign denotes the route, along a straight path between fields for 120m, to a kissing gate at the entrance to Nevis Forest.

3. Walk up the short path to meet a wider track, which you cross over then start ascending steeply up some steps that have a handrail at the side.

4. Continue on this steep ascent on a well-defined path through the forest to a kissing gate then on to a green post, which marks a turning off to the right leading to Cow Hill mast.

5. Turn right at the green post keeping on the stony path for 1.4km, crossing a stile then continuing on the undulating track leading to the mast, which you may see ahead, at G.R.113735, cloud permitting.

6. When you reach the mast, take care in low cloud, and do not venture too far away from the mast itself. Good views of Fort William and the surrounding area abound from here.

7. Return on the same route to the Visitor Centre remembering to turn left at the green post and taking extra care on the descent.

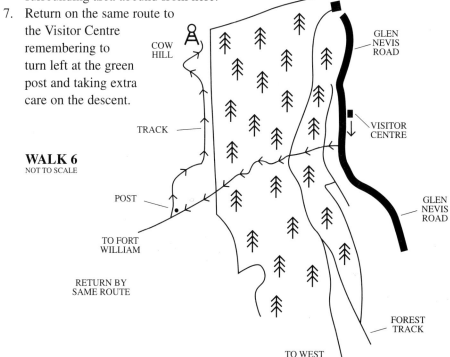

Walk 7:- Steall Falls

Start/Parking - Lower Falls car park G.R. 145683 (Lock valuables in car boot).

Distance - 6km (3.7 miles)   Time to allow - 1½hours

Terrain - Single track road then grass/stone path, can be slippery when wet.

Comment -A pleasant walk with good views of the river and a waterslide. The walk culminates in the spectacular Steall Falls waterfall in this hanging valley. This walk is not to be missed.

1. The Lower Falls car park is 200m past Achriabhach at the end of Nevis Forest.

2. Turn right out of the car park following the road over two small bridges with impressive waterfalls below. Stay on the road as you ascend for 2.4km to the Upper Falls car park where the road stops. Just before the car park you pass an impressive water slide cascading down the mountainside on your left.

3. The footpath to Steall Falls starts here. The path can be very slippery when wet as it often is. Initially the path is stony and rutted but well defined as you walk parallel with the river below in the Glen.

4. The path crosses two small waterfalls coming down the mountainside on your left. It may be difficult walking over the wet stones for part of the route here.

5. Cross another waterfall, where looking down into the Glen you can see the river racing over the rocks on its journey along the Glen. Take care on the path as there is a steep drop off to your right

6. You come to a high point on the path then you descend to a wooden platform before ascending over it. Hold the handrail as you pass.

7. Rounding a bend in the path you see the spectacular Steall Falls waterfall dropping into the river at the far end of this hanging valley.

8. On the opposite side of the river is a mountain rescue bothy. A rope bridge gives access to it. You have good views of Ben Nevis from here as you perhaps stop for a picnic before retracing your steps back to the car park.

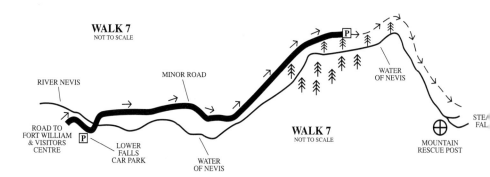

Walk 8:- Lochan Meall an t-Suidhe (a mountain loch on the Ben Nevis path)
Start - Opposite Glen Nevis Youth Hostel G.R.128717
Distance - 6.6km (4.1 miles)   Time to allow - 4hours
Parking - Lay-by near Glen Nevis Youth Hostel
Terrain - Very steep with a lot of loose stone on the path.
Comment - Very strenuous but worth the effort. Two steps forward and one back. Ensure you have suitable clothing and footwear for this walk.

1. Walk to the footbridge crossing the River Nevis opposite the youth hostel, cross the bridge then cross a fence with steps over it. An information board displays the current weather conditions on Ben Nevis.

2. Continue on the path, which now starts to ascend steeply as it twists around the mountainside. You join a path from the left, but you keep right, still ascending the main Ben Nevis path.

3. You pass a seat on your ascent, then go over two small metal bridges on this extremely stony route. The path ascends along the side of Red Burn where you can hear the noise of the water rushing down the mountainside.

4. Just before reaching the loch, you see a conservation sign as you are ascending steeply.

5. Reaching the loch and hanging valley, the path levels out and is often very wet with natural springs. The area is exposed and can be inhospitable in bad weather but is an enjoyable picnic stop in good conditions.

6. Stay on the path to a sharp right hand bend then bear left towards the loch. There are numerous large stones to sit on, where there are good views in all directions.

7. You should return by the same route to the youth hostel.

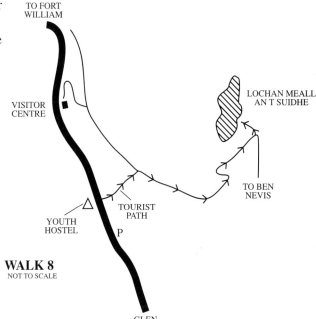

TO FORT
WILLIAM

VISITOR
CENTRE

LOCHAN MEALL
AN T SUIDHE

TO BEN
NEVIS

TOURIST
PATH

YOUTH
HOSTEL

P

WALK 8
NOT TO SCALE

GLEN
NEVIS

Walk 9:- Nevis Bridge Walk (circular)

Start/Parking - Glen Nevis Visitors Centre G.R.123730

Distance - 8.1km (5 miles)   **Time to Allow - 3hours**

Terrain - A steep ascent from the youth hostel, then undulating stony track followed by single track road and forest track.

Comment - A pleasant walk in varying surroundings.

1. Leaving the Visitor Centre car park, turn left walking along the footpath for 1.4km to the youth hostel.
2. Cross the bridge opposite the youth hostel then go over some steps to an information board showing weather conditions on Ben Nevis.
3. Ascend steeply on a path, which winds around the hillside until you join another path from your left, coming from the Visitor Centre.
4. Turn left here and descend a stony path to a farm track beside a stone wall.
5. Bear right along this track to a small wood 200m further ahead where there is a car parking area next to it.
6. Continue on the undulating single-track road for 2km, passing houses and an electricity sub station. You come to a junction with a sign pointing to Achintee path.
7. Look on your left near the junction for the small footbridge across the River Nevis. Cross this then turn left on the Glen Nevis road, walking on the footpath to a car park on your right at the entrance to the forest.
8. Follow the sign for forest walk, going through a gate to ascend a wide track into the forest. Continue for 1.2km to a path turning left near a waymark sign.
9. Turn left here descending to a kissing gate then along a path for 120m to the main road again.
10. Turn left at the main road, walking for 100m to the small entrance into the Visitor Centre on the opposite side of the road.

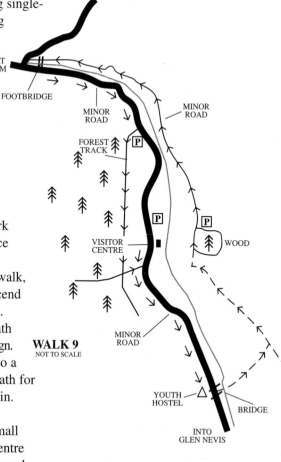

Walk 10:- Dun Deardail Fort

Start/Parking - Glen Nevis Visitor Centre G.R.123730
Distance - 8.2km (5.1 miles)   Time to allow - 2½hours
Terrain - Good forest track ascending gradually then a short path to the fort with two short but steep ascents.
Comments - Another walk with spectacular views throughout. Demanding in parts of the upper section.

1. Starting at the door of the Visitor Centre walk round to the road, turn left, walking for 230m to a sign on the opposite side pointing to The West Highland Way.

2. Turn right here along a straight path, to a kissing gate. Go through, ascend to a wide track with a small waymark sign again to The West Highland Way.

3. Follow this sign turning left to walk 700m to another sign at a fork in the track.

4. Turn off to the right following the sign and ascend through the forest on The West Highland Way. In the upper stages you go around two sharp bends on the track to a waymark post with a yellow arrow pointing up a narrow path to your right.

5. Ascend this path to a deer fence with a stile.

6. Go over, turning left along a line of trees on a narrow undulating path to the fort remains. The views from the summit are outstanding in all directions.

7. Retrace your steps, walking back through the forest to where your wide track joins another wide track at the lower end of the forest.

8. Turn right here walking for 400m to a metalled road section before turning left along a narrow path leading to a kissing gate.

9. Walk through then go between the houses onto a metalled road leading down to the main road beside the Glen Nevis Restaurant.

10. Turn left at the main road and walk for 1.1km on the footpath to the Visitor Centre.

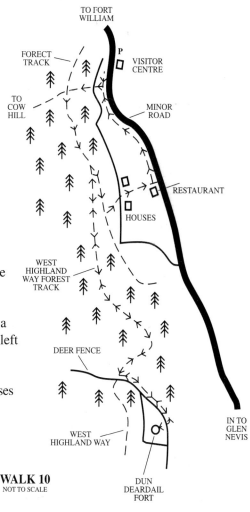

WALK 10
NOT TO SCALE

DUN
DEARDAIL
FORT

Walk 11:- Inverlochy Castle (circular)
Start/Parking - Glen Nevis Visitor Centre G.R.123730
Distance - 8.2km (5.1 miles)   Time to allow - 2¾hours
Terrain - Majority on footpath/metalled road with 2 sections on grass/path.
Comment - An easy walk with only one ascent near the beginning.

1. Leave the Visitor Centre by walking on a path north along by the river to a suspension bridge near the car park.
2. Cross the bridge following the sign for Ben path then pass Achintee (B&B) on your left. The Visitor Centre is now on the opposite side of the river.
3. You come to some steps over a fence where a sign points left to 'Ben path'. Cross here walking on a straight path for 250m to some steps in a stone wall.
4. Climb the steps then turn left on a stony farm track towards the farm and wood walking for 200m to the single track metalled road.
5. Continue on this undulating road for 2km passing an electricity sub station on your right, with houses on your left.
6. You come to a junction with a sign pointing back to Achintee path. Turn left here, walking a short distance to the main A82 road.
7. Turn right now, passing the Ben Nevis industrial estate and walking for 1.2km to a minor road on your left leading to Inverlochy Castle. A sign is at the junction. Walk around the bend to the castle and explore this interesting ruin.
8. Turn right on the road at the side of the castle, walking down a short lane and under a railway bridge.
9. Cross a stile on your right into a field and follow the grass path along the riverbank, crossing a wide water channel as you go towards Inverlochy.
10. On reaching the houses walk along by the village shops to some traffic lights.
11. Turn right, walking to the small roundabout at the entrance to Glen Nevis.
12. Turn left here, walking on the footpath for 2km back to the Visitor Centre.

INVERLOCHY CASTLE
RIVER LOCHY
TO INVERNESS
A82 ROAD
HOUSES
HOUSES
TO FORT WILLIAM
GLEN NEVIS ROAD
WALK 11
NOT TO SCALE
P
VISITORS CENTRE
ROAD
WOO
GLEN NEVIS

Walk 12:- Scotch Whisky Trail (Ben Nevis Distillery)
Start/Parking - Car park, north end of Glen Nevis Forest G.R.122737
Distance - 10km (6.2 miles)   Time to allow - 3hours
Terrain - Footpath/road with a gradual ascent but mostly flat.
Comment - A good walk with refreshment at the distillery!

1. Turn left from the car park, walking on the footpath to the roundabout at the entrance to Glen Nevis.
2. At this roundabout turn right, walking on the A82 for 2km to the traffic lights at the junction with the A83 road and passing Ben Nevis industrial estate on your right.
3. Walk straight across the lights and the distillery is on your right 100m further. The distillery is open most days for visits, showing the history of whisky making in Fort William and other interesting items as well as offering refreshments.
4. Leaving the distillery, turn left retracing your steps to the last turning on your left before the Glen Nevis roundabout.
5. After passing the industrial estate again turn left then right following the signs to Achintee path.
6. Gradually ascend on a single-track road to a wood and farm at Achintee.
7. Walk along the track ahead for 200m to some steps over a stone wall on your right.
8. Go over then descend a straight path to a stile near the River Nevis.
9. Cross the stile and turn right to the suspension bridge ahead of you.
10. Cross the bridge to go through the Visitor Centre car park to the main Glen Nevis road.
11. Turn right walking for 900m back to the car park at the end of the forest.

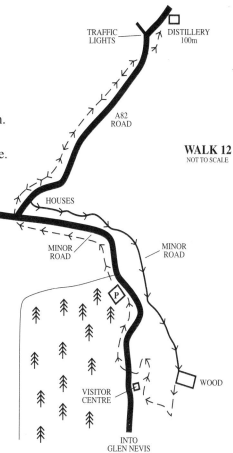

Walk 13:- Stob Ban

Start - Glen Nevis Visitor Centre G.R.123730
Distance - A/21.1km B/10.5km Time to allow - A/7½hrs B/4½hrs
Parking - A/Glen Nevis Visitor Centre B/Lower Falls car park G.R.145683
Terrain - Forest track and old stalkers path, loose stone at high level.
Comment - Extremely strenuous and demanding, some steep ascents over loose stone. Ensure you have appropriate clothing and equipment to tackle this one.

1A From the Visitor Centre, turn left, walk into Glen Nevis, passing the campsite and youth hostel on your right. The footpath stops at the youth hostel so walk on the right side until you reach the Lower Falls car park.

1B Park here if travelling by car. Walk past the car park to the first stile on your right, a sign states 'sheep graze here', G.R.145684.

2. Your path is initially grass and stone and a gradual climb to Allt Coire a`Mhusgain at G.R.150673.

3. After the wooded section, the path turns left ascending steeply then zigzags sharply. Follow the main path carefully, do not venture onto any offshoots of the main path.

4. The path finally turns right where, looking back along the Glen the views are outstanding. Cross the burn and ascend to the saddle between Stob Ban and Sgorr an Lubhair.

5. Reaching the saddle you join another path running across left to right. Off to the left is the mountain loch known as Lochan Coire nam Miseach, a good picnic stop.

6. Your path to Stob Ban summit turns right at the junction before going straight ahead (do not turn down left). There is a lot of loose stone and scree here and it can be an effort to scramble over it.

7. A cairn marks the summit and you are amply rewarded for your effort with outstanding views.

8. Returning to Glen Nevis, retrace your path back to the Lower Falls, taking care on the scree and winding paths.

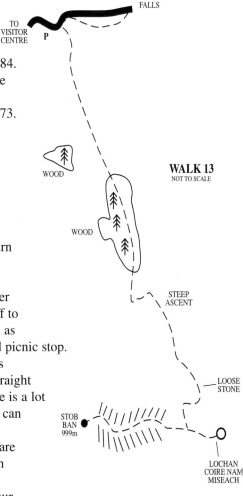

Walk 14:- Cow Hill Mast via Fort William (circular)
Start/Parking - Glen Nevis Visitor Centre G.R.123730
Distance - 11.5km (7.2miles)   Time to allow - 4hours
Terrain - Footpath/stony track with a gradual ascent followed by a steep descent
Comment - Views from the summit are exceptional, take a camera.
I recommend you do this walk in the direction stated, as the ascent is very steep in reverse.

1. From the Visitor Centre, turn right and walk on the footpath to the roundabout at the entrance to Glen Nevis. Continue into Fort William centre, walking along the main street to the roundabout near the police station, a total of 4.4km.
2. Turn left at this roundabout and ascend Lundavra Road through the housing estate following the sign at the roundabout for Upper Auchintore. Pass houses on both sides as you walk to the cattle grid at the top of the road.
3. Past the cattle grid is a 5 bar gate on your left and a notice states 'access needed at all times'. Walk through the space at the side of the gate on a firm but stony track leading to Cow Hill mast. There are good views of Ben Nevis and surrounding area.
4. The track winds around the hillside before coming to a green post with a path leading off right. Keep on the main track going over a stile next to a 5 bar gate then winding round to the mast ahead.
5. Take care not to venture too far away from the mast especially in low visibility.
6. Leaving the mast, retrace your steps back to the green post now on your left, that you passed earlier. Turn left onto a path, which leads to a kissing gate, before descending steeply through the forest.
7. You come to a wide track crossing your path below. There is a handrail down some steps there. Cross straight over the track to another kissing gate then along a straight path for 120m to the Glen Nevis road.
8. Turn left, then first right back into the Visitor Centre on the opposite side.

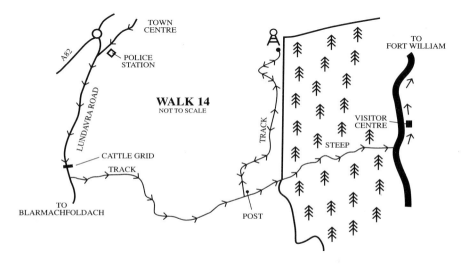

Walk 15:- River Nevis Walk (long, circular)

Start/Parking - Glen Nevis Visitor Centre G.R.123730
Distance - 12km (7.5miles)   Time to allow - 4½hours
Terrain - Flat path easy to follow at first, becoming wet in numerous parts and more testing.
Comment - A pleasant walk by the river but can be wet towards the end of the Glen. Generally keep on the path by the river to the end of the Glen.

1. Walk to the suspension bridge at the Visitor Centre. Cross the bridge following the sign there for 'Ben path'. Continue along the riverbank passing Achintee Farm (B&B) on your left. You see the Visitor Centre on the other side.

2. At a turning left for the Ben path, carry straight on by the river. Cross four burns leading into the river before coming to a footbridge over the river near the youth hostel. Do not cross the bridge but continue along the riverbank path passing a stile on your left beside the bridge, leading up to Ben Nevis.

3. Walk around a wire fence, past another stile, cross a burn then a stile following a path to another stile at the far end of a field. This takes you back onto the main riverbank path.

4. Further on cross another stile into a large field on your left following a feint path initially beside the fence going towards a square of trees ahead. This is an ancient burial ground of the Cameron's used in 1700.

5. At the far side of the trees turn right to a 5 bar gate near the river, then turn left again on the path. It becomes more difficult to walk on the path as it crosses several burns before going through a wood.

6. Cross two boggy sections as the path becomes progressively harder to walk along, before ascending towards two white buildings. Walk up the steps at the side of the first building to a farm track.

7. Turn right, walking along the track, to go through two 5 bar gates at the side of a sheep pen, then through another onto the metalled road.

8. Turn right crossing two small bridges following the road around to the right as you pass the Lower Falls car park. Cross another small bridge at Achriabhach, then turn left onto a wide track through the forest going through a 5 bar gate. Do not take the narrow path ascending the side of the forest.

9. Continue for 6km through the forest, do not deviate from this path but stay on the track until you come to a path crossing left to right. then walk 120m to the main Glen Nevis road.

11. Turn left then after a short distance turn right back to the Visitor Centre.

TO VISITOR CENTRE

OLD BURIAL GROUND

SKETCH OF MIDDLE SECTION

RIVER NEVIS

FOREST TRACK

GLEN NEVIS ROAD

WALK 15
NOT TO SCALE

RIVER

2 COTTAGES

BRIDGE

ACHRIABHACH

Walk 16:- Neptune's Staircase (circular)
Start/Parking - Glen Nevis Visitor Centre G.R.123730
Distance - 13km (8.1miles)   **Time to allow - 3¼hours**
Terrain - One short ascent with most of the route on footpath
Comment - Gain an insight into how a flight of locks work, which should be very interesting. Take care not to fall in the lock.

1. Pick up the path along by the riverbank and walk to the suspension bridge near the car park. Cross the bridge following the sign for 'Ben path'.

2. Just past the Achintee guesthouse turn left, again following the 'Ben path' sign.

3. Ascend the straight path to a stone wall 250m further on. Cross the steps over the wall then turn left on a track leading to a parking area near Achintee Farm.

4. Walk along the undulating road for 2km, passing houses at the lower end. At a road junction a sign points back to Achintee path, turn left to the main A82 road.

5. Turn right at the A82 and walk to the traffic lights, passing the Ben Nevis industrial estate on your right. Take care on the busy roads.

6. At the traffic lights turn left onto the A830, cross the River Lochy, walking on a straight road for 1.3km to a swing bridge over the Caledonian Canal. A gate at the side of the canal leads to the flight of locks. There are 8 in total and you can watch the boats passing through on their journey to Inverness. The canal has been in use since 1822 and runs for 60miles, passing through Loch Ness.

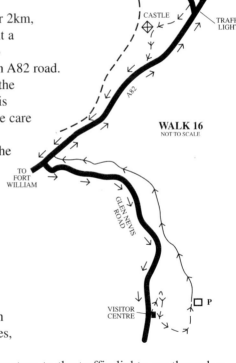

7. Leaving the lock area, retrace your steps to the traffic lights, go through a gate on your right onto a path taking you past a pitch and putt and a football field on your left, with the river on your right. Just past Inverlochy Castle turn left on a road back to the A82 road.

8. Turn right, walking to the Nevis Bridge roundabout 1.2km further on.

9. Turn left walking on the footpath for 2km back to Glen Nevis Visitor Centre.

Walk 17:- Blarmachfoldach (circular)

Start/Parking - Glen Nevis Visitor Centre G.R.123730

Distance - 19.7km (12.2miles)   Time to allow - 5½hours

Terrain - Well-defined undulating track/path then a 6km walk on metalled road.

Comment - Moderately difficult with some short steep climbs.

1. Turn left from the Visitor Centre, cross the road walking to a sign 230m along the road for West Highland Way, just before the white house (B&B) on the right.

2. Turn onto a path towards the forest, go through a kissing gate, and then ascend a short path to meet a wide track. Follow waymark sign for West Highland Way to the left.

3. You are now on a good track through the forest, 700m further on turn right, ascending another wide track to the upper forest area.

4. There are good views of the Ben and Glen Nevis to your left. Continue for 1.7km rounding two hairpin bends in the path. Look for a waymark sign on your right at the end of the track, which points along a narrow path to your right. Continue ascending steeply for a short distance to a fence and stile.

5. Cross the stile, continue on the obvious path on The West Highland Way. Walk through a large forest for 3.2km, cross over five deer fences and pass through a firebreak in the forest.

6. Stay on this path through the second part of the forest section before crossing open grassland for 1km. Walk through a 600m section of forest before coming to a seat on your right with a signboard nearby.

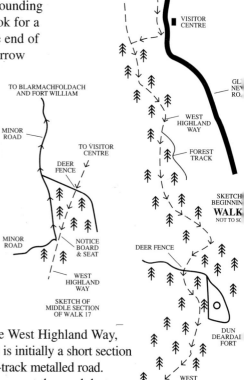

7. Turn right at the signboard off The West Highland Way, onto Caulfields Military Road. This is initially a short section of rough track followed by a single-track metalled road.

8. Do not take the left turn where you meet the road, but continue ahead for 6.1km through Blarmachfoldach towards Fort William. Cross two cattle grids on the undulating road, eventually coming to the top of Lundavra Road above Fort William.

9. Descend the hill through to the roundabout near Fort William police station.

10. Turn right on the main street, walking to the roundabout at the entrance to Glen Nevis. Walk straight across into Glen Nevis, continuing along the footpath for 2km back to the Visitor Centre.